D1251126

The Atlas of
Famous Battles
of the American
Revolution ™

The Battle of Saratoga

Wendy Vierow

The Rosen Publishing Group's
PowerKids Press ™
New York

To Chris, who loves maps

Published in 2003 by The Rosen Publishing Group, Inc.
29 East 21st Street, New York, NY 10010

Copyright © 2003 by The Rosen Publishing Group, Inc.

All rights reserved. No part of this book may be reproduced in any form without permission in writing from the publisher, except by a reviewer.

First Edition

Editor: Nancy MacDonell Smith

Book Design: Michael J. Caroleo

Picture Credits: Cover, title page, pp. 11–12, 15–16 (maps), Maria Melendez; cover, title page, p. 7 (Burgoyne) Architect of the Capitol; cover, title page, p. 8 (Gates) Independence National Historic Park; p. 4 (map) Map Division, Library of Congress; pp. 4 (left), 12 (bottom), 16 (inset and bottom), 19 (inset), 20 (left and inset) Dover Pictorial Archive Series; p. 4 (inset) © North Wind Picture Archives; p. 7 (inset) © David Muench/CORBIS; p. 7 (bottom right) © CORBIS; pp.7–8 (maps) Nick Sciacca; p.8 (cannon) Lee Snider; Lee Snider/CORBIS; p. 8 (top left) © Bettmann/CORBIS; pp. 12 (pistol, rifle),15 (powder horn), 16 (saber),19 (hatchet, caltrop) courtesy the George C. Neumann Collection, Valley Forge National Historic Park, photos by Cindy Reiman; p. 15 (inset) SuperStock, Inc.; pp. 19–20 (maps) Colin Dizengoff.

Vierow, Wendy.
  The Battle of Saratoga / Wendy Vierow.— 1st ed.
      p. cm. — (The atlas of famous battles of the American Revolution)
  Includes bibliographical references and index.
  ISBN 0-8239-6332-2 (library binding)
  1. Saratoga Campaign, 1777—Juvenile literature. [1. Saratoga Campaign, 1777. 2. United States—History—Revolution, 1775–1783—Campaigns.] I. Title. II. Series.
  E241.S2 V54 2003
  973.3'33—dc21

                                                                                      2001007779

Manufactured in the United States of America

Contents

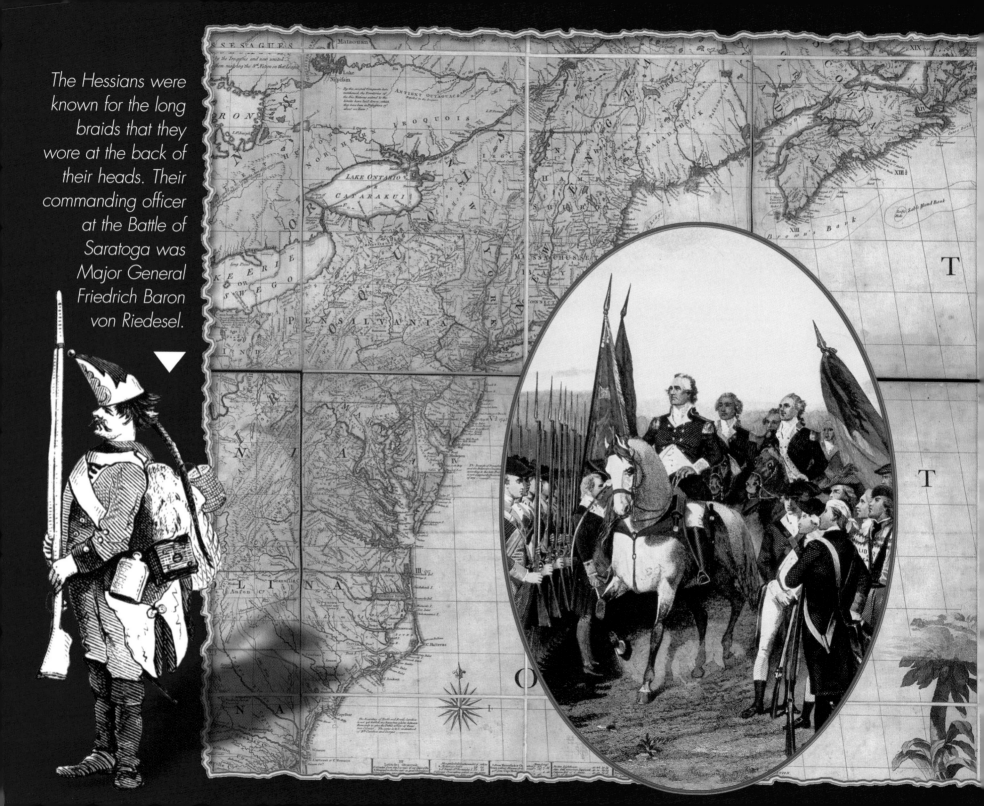

The Hessians were known for the long braids that they wore at the back of their heads. Their commanding officer at the Battle of Saratoga was Major General Friedrich Baron von Riedesel.

A Revolution Begins

The Battle of Saratoga, fought in the fall of 1777, was the first major battle won by the Americans in the **American Revolution**. The Battle of Saratoga was really two separate battles. It was a turning point in the Revolution because it showed that the Americans might win the fight against Great Britain.

From 1775 until 1777, Great Britain had many advantages against the Americans. It had a large army, the world's greatest navy, and the money needed to fight a war. The British paid German soldiers, called **Hessians**, to fight with them in battles, including at Saratoga. In contrast, the Americans had a smaller, untrained army, no navy, and little money. However, by the Battle of Saratoga, American soldiers had learned to fight well. The Americans also had an excellent leader, General George Washington. He was the commander in chief of the **Continental army**.

This map of the 13 colonies dates from the time of the American Revolution. The Battle of Saratoga was fought in what is now northeastern New York State. **Inset:** *General Washington was a skilled farmer, businessman, and soldier.*

The British Make a Plan

British lieutenant general John Burgoyne wanted to control the **Hudson River valley**. Burgoyne was an experienced British soldier and politician. He believed that if the British could control the Hudson River valley, they could cut off New England's colonies and New York from the other colonies. In this way, the British hoped to win the war. As one of the steps to controlling the Hudson River valley, Burgoyne and his troops planned to capture Albany, New York. British general William Howe and his troops were to meet Burgoyne in Albany. Howe was the commander in chief of the British military. He was the second person to be commander in chief of the British forces since the war began. The previous commander was replaced because he could not defeat the Americans. The plan to capture Albany did not succeed. It was interrupted by two battles near the town of Saratoga, New York.

*General Burgoyne planned to move south down Lake Champlain to Albany. General Howe's troops were supposed to march north to Albany. Each group was made up of about 10,000 troops. **Inset:** This photo shows the Hudson River as seen from Saratoga. **Top:** General Burgoyne became a soldier when he was just 15. **Bottom:** This is an illustration of General William Howe.*

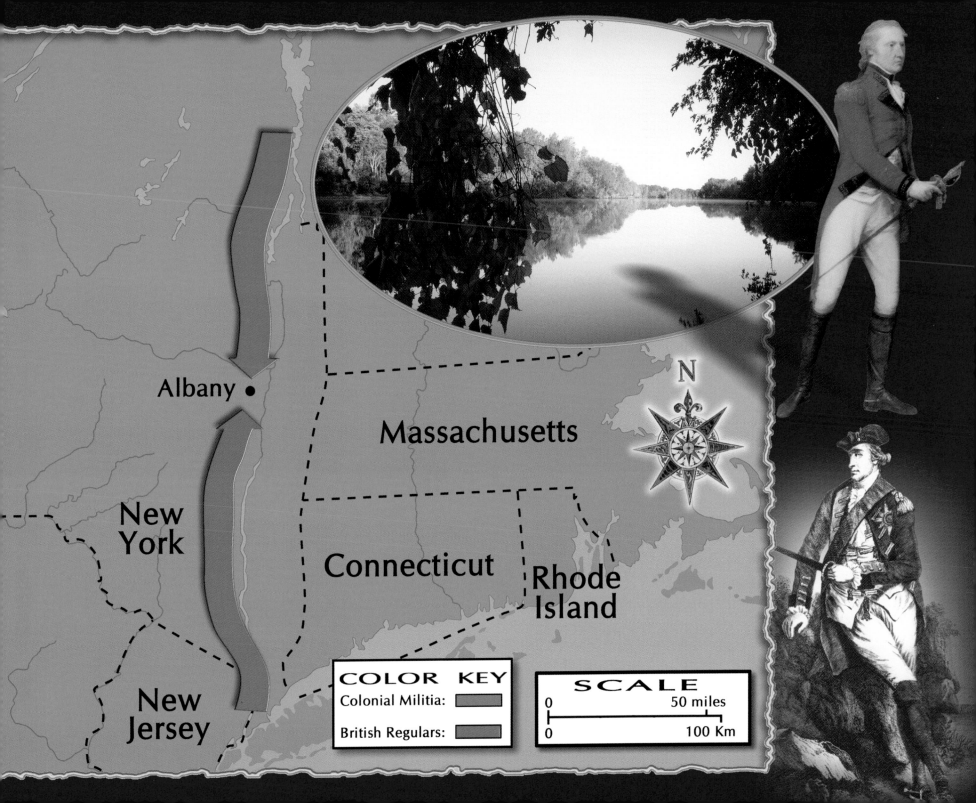

Albany •

Massachusetts

N

New York

Connecticut

Rhode Island

New Jersey

COLOR KEY	
Colonial Militia:	
British Regulars:	

SCALE	
0	50 miles
0	100 Km

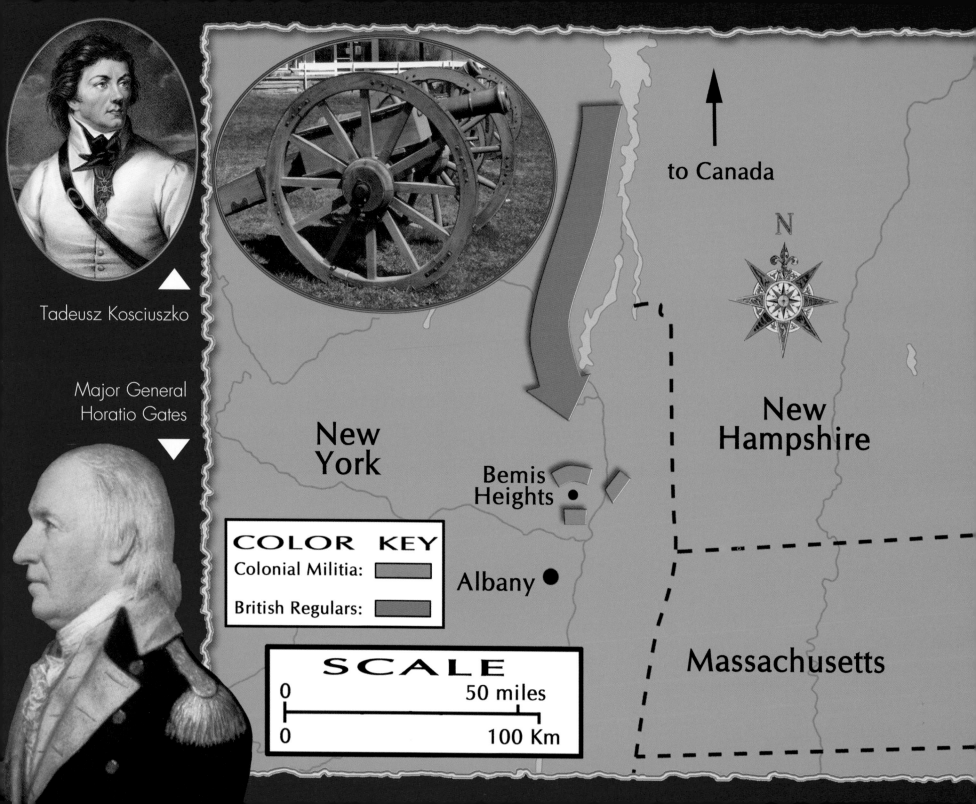

Tadeusz Kosciuszko

Major General
Horatio Gates

to Canada

N

New
York

New
Hampshire

Bemis
Heights

Albany

Massachusetts

COLOR KEY

Colonial Militia:

British Regulars:

SCALE

0   50 miles

0   100 Km

The British March Toward Albany

In the summer of 1777, Burgoyne began to march with his troops from Canada toward Albany. Burgoyne's troops included British, German, Canadian, Native American, and American **loyalist** soldiers. Many American **patriots** destroyed bridges so that Burgoyne's troops could not cross streams. The British moved slowly. They had to stop to build bridges so that their large guns and carts could cross the streams. This gave American troops, under Major General Horatio Gates, time to get ready for the British. Though he was an American general, Gates was born in England and had served in the British army as a boy. At that time, boys as young as 10 years old could join the army.

The Americans were helped by Tadeusz Kosciuszko, a Polish officer and military **engineer** serving with the Americans. He told them to put cannons on the road to Albany near Bemis Heights in what is now New York State. Americans also put guns in **redoubts** that they built nearby.

It took General Burgoyne and his men most of the summer of 1777 to reach Saratoga from St. John's, Canada, a distance of about 160 miles (257 km). **Inset:** *This British cannon was used at the Battle of Saratoga. The cannon is still there today.*

British and American Troops Meet

On September 13, 1777, British general Burgoyne and his soldiers began to cross the Hudson River at the town of Saratoga, New York. Today, Saratoga is known as Schuylerville. The British were headed toward Albany. It took them two days to cross the river. Finally the troops began their march toward Albany.

On September 16, 1777, Burgoyne heard the sound of drums. He thought that the drums must belong to American soldiers. He sent a group of British soldiers to try to find the Americans. His soldiers found tracks leading to an empty farm, called Freeman's Farm. Some British soldiers went to the farm to find food. On September 17, 1777, American soldiers who were patrolling Freeman's Farm discovered British soldiers digging up potatoes. The Americans killed and wounded several of the British soldiers. They also took 20 British soldiers as prisoners.

Once the British and the Hessians crossed the Hudson River, they began to make their way through the woods toward Albany. **Inset:** *These are two differently dressed American soldiers. On the right is an officer from the First Rhode Island Regiment, and to the left is a private from Colonel Seth Warner's Green Mountain Boys.*

to Albany

to Saratoga

Hudson River

Freeman's Farm

COLOR KEY

Colonial Militia:

British Regulars:

This American soldier was a private in the Rifle Regiment of Pennsylvania.

This carbine rifle was used by a British soldier during the American Revolution.

Battles were often fought in open fields, but there were many trees at Saratoga.

COLOR KEY

Colonial Militia:

British Regulars:

to Albany

Freeman's Farm

The First Battle of Saratoga

The British decided to attack the Americans. On September 19, 1777, they marched toward the Americans in three separate groups. Americans met with one of these groups at Freeman's Farm. Because the British had broken up into small groups, the first group of British soldiers fighting the Americans was outnumbered. The Americans and the British fought for about three hours. The British fought as soldiers did in Europe, lined up in the open. The Americans fought while hiding behind trees and other objects. They had learned these fighting **techniques** from Native Americans. Finally the two other groups of British soldiers arrived. The Americans fell back as night came. At the end of the day, the British were able to hold their ground at Freeman's Farm. This became known as the First Battle of Saratoga, or the Battle of Freeman's Farm. The British losses in the battle were great. There were 600 killed or wounded British soldiers. The American losses totaled 319 killed or wounded men.

Many of the British that were killed at Freeman's Farm were officers. **Top:** *The screw-barrel pistol was used by officers in the eighteenth century. The end of the pistol was screwed off to load it.* **Bottom:** *Officers directed the battle from a high point, where they could easily see the fighting.*

The British Wait for Help

General Burgoyne had lost many soldiers in the fight at Freeman's Farm on September 19, 1777. He decided to wait for help rather than to continue fighting. Burgoyne hoped that more British troops would come to help him fight the Americans. While they were waiting for help, Burgoyne's troops built redoubts and **trenches** to protect themselves. The three redoubts that they built were called the Great Redoubt, the Balcarres Redoubt, and the Breymann Redoubt. For three weeks, Burgoyne waited for more British troops. However, help never arrived.

Burgoyne and his troops were running out of food. Their horses were dying from hunger. Many British soldiers ran away, leaving Burgoyne with only 5,000 British soldiers. The Americans stayed at Bemis Heights. They also stayed near Fort Neilson, close to Bemis Heights. During this time, 3,000 more American soldiers and **militia** members joined the fight. They began to fire on the British.

At Bemis Heights, 11,000 American soldiers had gathered by the end of the first week in October.
Inset: The Continental army wasn't large enough to fight the British on its own. General Washington used both regular and volunteer soldiers.

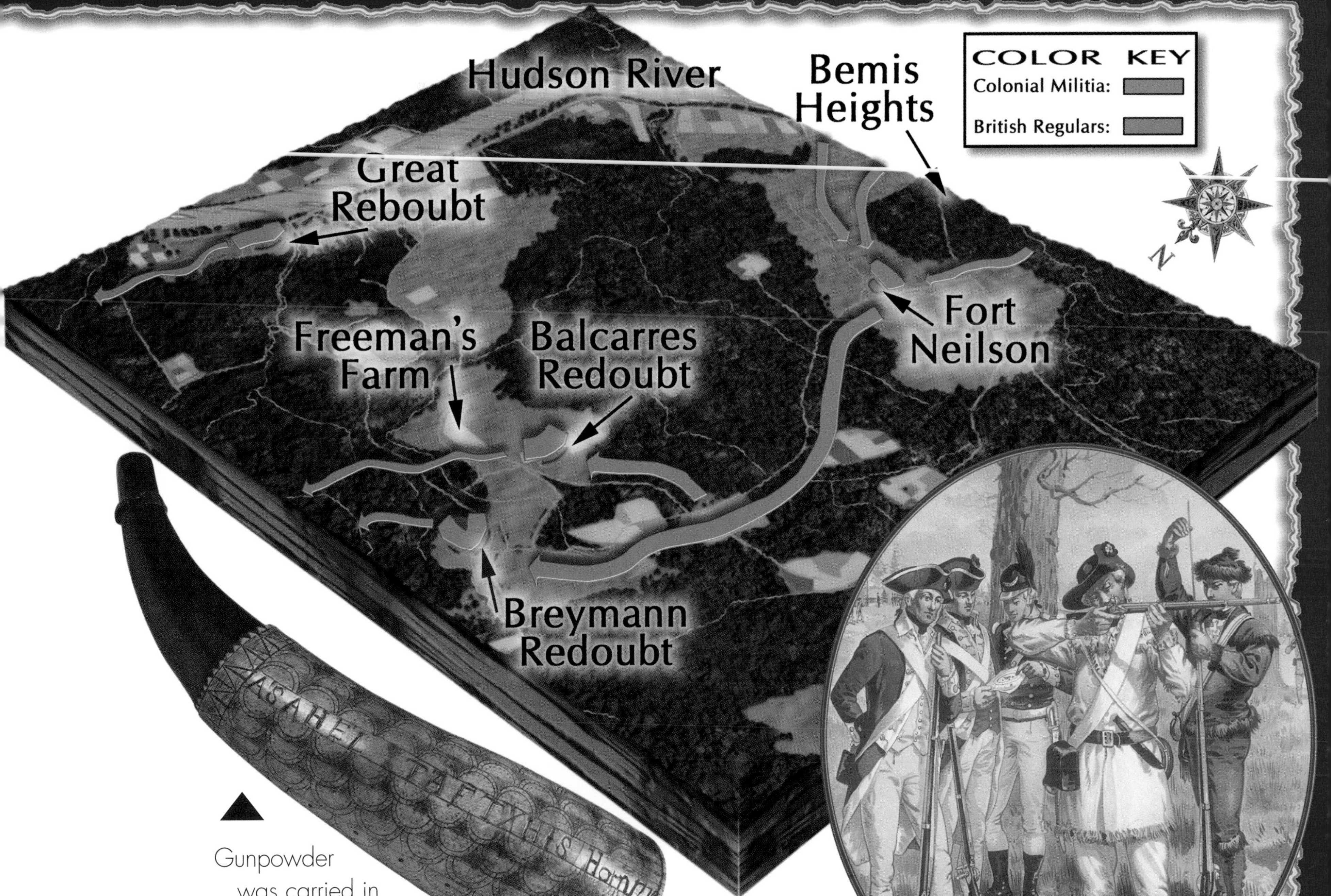

Hudson River

Bemis Heights

COLOR KEY

Colonial Militia:

British Regulars:

Great Reboubt

Freeman's Farm

Balcarres Redoubt

Fort Neilson

Breymann Redoubt

Gunpowder was carried in powder horns.

COLOR KEY
Colonial Militia:
British Regulars:

Balcarres
Redoubt

Freeman's
Farm

Breymann
Redoubt

Barber
Farm

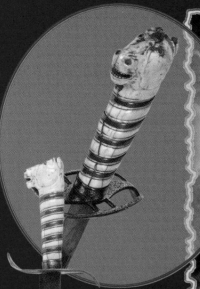

Officers carried fancy swords. This one has an ivory handle carved to look like a horse's head.

The Second Battle of Saratoga

On October 7, 1777, General Burgoyne decided that he could wait no longer for help. He sent a group of British troops to find out what the American soldiers were doing. The British troops spread out in a field at Barber Farm. The American troops at the **outposts** noticed the British activity. General Gates ordered the Americans to attack the British.

American general Benedict Arnold decided to attack a group of German troops that were fighting for the British. The Americans fought well. The Germans, along with many British, **retreated** and headed for Freeman's Farm. Arnold and the American troops then attacked the Balcarres Redoubt, but they could not capture it. Next, Arnold and the Americans attacked the Breymann Redoubt, where more German soldiers were fighting. The Americans captured that redoubt. The fighting of October 7, 1777, became known as the Second Battle of Saratoga, or the Battle of Bemis Heights. Bemis Heights was the location of the battle.

The American losses at the Second Battle of Saratoga totaled 150 men killed or wounded. The British losses totaled 600 men killed or wounded. **Inset:** *German foot soldiers were driven back by Americans on horseback.* **Bottom:** *General Arnold was one of the officers in the field that day.*

Americans Surround the British

On the night of October 7, 1777, British troops stayed near the Great Redoubt. The next day, American troops moved into the empty British camp near the Great Redoubt. General Burgoyne decided that the best thing to do was to retreat north with his British soldiers. On the night of October 8, 1777, the British began to move north. During the retreat, it rained heavily. The next morning, the British found that many American soldiers had taken positions on the east side of the Hudson River. This prevented the British from escaping east across the Hudson River. The Americans were on both sides of the Hudson River.

The British soon discovered that Americans were blocking the roads that led north so that an escape was impossible. American soldiers, numbering close to 20,000, surrounded the British. The 5,000 British soldiers were tired and starving. There was no escape.

*Following the Second Battle of Saratoga, the British were trapped by American troops. After meeting with his officers, General Burgoyne decided to give up. **Inset:** To stop the British from escaping, the Americans chopped down trees and used the logs to block the roads.*

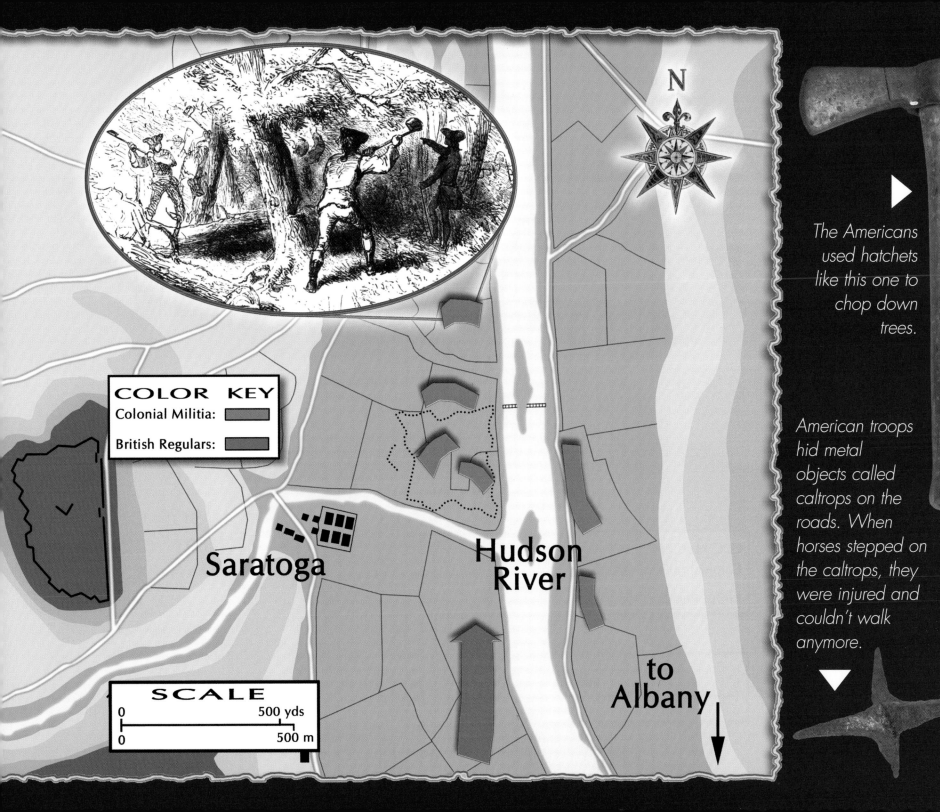

COLOR KEY

Colonial Militia:

British Regulars:

Saratoga

Hudson River

to Albany

N

SCALE

0 — 500 yds

0 — 500 m

The Americans used hatchets like this one to chop down trees.

American troops hid metal objects called caltrops on the roads. When horses stepped on the caltrops, they were injured and couldn't walk anymore.

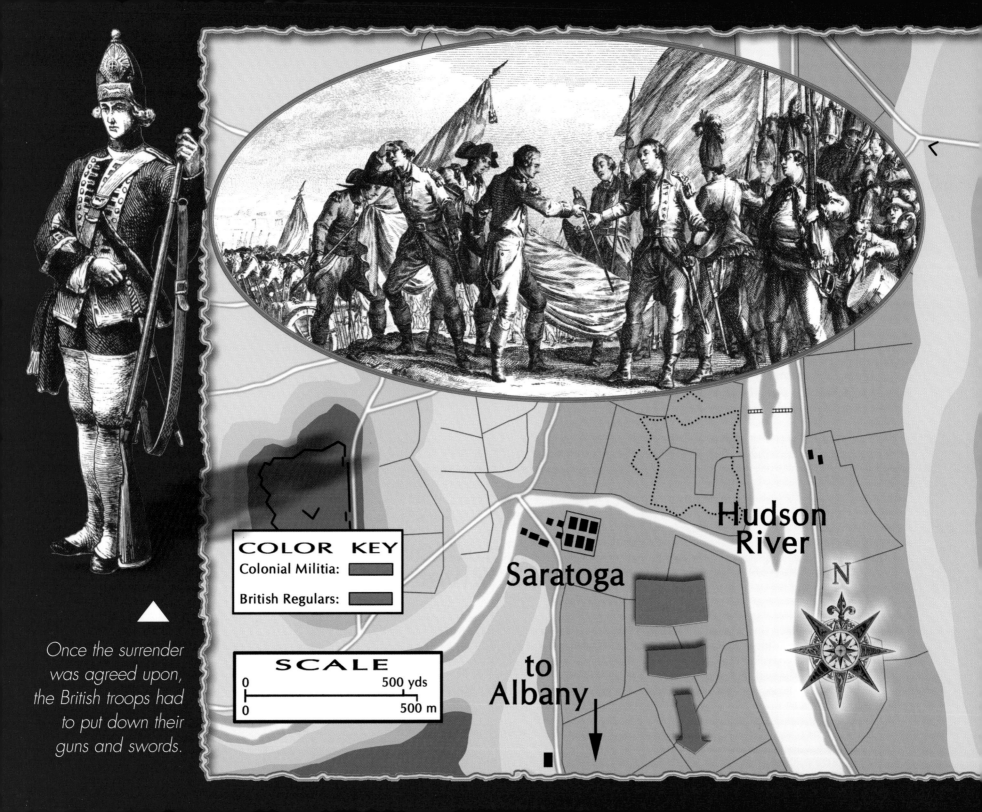

Once the surrender was agreed upon, the British troops had to put down their guns and swords.

COLOR KEY

Colonial Militia:

British Regulars:

SCALE

0   500 yds

0   500 m

Saratoga

to Albany

Hudson River

N

The British Give Up the Fight

On October 13, 1777, General Burgoyne sent General Gates a message of **surrender**. The two generals discussed the terms of surrender. On October 17, the two generals agreed that the British troops would give up their weapons and would be allowed to return to Great Britain. However, they would not be allowed to return to America to fight in the American Revolution. Although these soldiers could not fight in America, Britain could still send other soldiers to fight in the Revolution.

At 2:00 P.M. the next afternoon, the British surrendered to the Americans. British soldiers stacked their weapons along the west bank of the Hudson River. Then, as was the custom, General Burgoyne and General Gates had dinner together.

Burgoyne and his troops returned to Great Britain. Burgoyne had lost an important battle. He was never given another army to command.

After surrendering on the west bank of the Hudson River, British troops began the 200-mile (322-km) march to Boston, where they would board ships to return to Great Britain. **Inset:** *General Burgoyne surrendered on behalf of his troops. Burgoyne was then taken to Albany.*

The French Join the Americans

The Battle of Saratoga was an important American victory. Leaders of other countries heard that the American army had beaten the British army. The Americans had also forced part of the British army to leave America.

In France, people were **impressed** that the Americans had won the Battle of Saratoga. They began to realize that the Americans could win the war. French leaders thought that a partnership with the United States would be a good idea. About three months after the Battle of Saratoga, France promised to help the United States. France became an **ally** of the United States. Soon French soldiers fought beside American soldiers in the American Revolution.

The Battle of Saratoga was a turning point in the Revolution because it resulted in a **partnership** with France. With the help of France and other countries, the Americans won the war against Great Britain in 1783.

Glossary

ally (A-ly) A country that supports another country.

American Revolution (uh-MER-uh-ken reh-vuh-LOO-shun) Battles that soldiers from the American colonies fought against Britain for freedom, from 1775 to 1783.

Continental army (kon-tin-EN-tul AR-mee) The army of patriots created in 1775, with George Washington as its commander in chief.

engineer (en-jih-NEER) Someone who is an expert at planning and building engines, machines, roads, bridges, and canals.

Hessians (HEH-shenz) German soldiers who were paid to fight for the British during the American Revolution.

Hudson River valley (HUD-son RIH-ver VA-lee) The area on either side of the Hudson River north of New York City.

impressed (im-PREST) Made a strong effect on the mind or feelings.

loyalist (LOY-uh-list) A person who is loyal to a certain political party, government, or ruler.

militia (muh-LIH-shuh) A group of people who are trained and ready to fight in an emergency.

outposts (OWT-pohsts) Military camps that are set up away from the main camp to warn against surprise attacks.

partnership (PART-ner-ship) When two or more people join together for a cause.

patriots (PAY-tree-uhts) People who love and defend their country.

redoubts (rih-DOWTS) Small forts outside fortifications to defend the gates.

retreated (ree-TREET-ed) Moved back from a difficult situation.

surrender (suh-REN-der) To give up a fight or battle.

techniques (tek-NEEKS) Special methods or systems used to do something.

trenches (TRENCH-ez) Long pits dug in the ground where soldiers hid to shoot at an enemy.

Index

Primary Sources

Cover (right) and page 7 (top). *Surrender of Burgoyne.* Oil on canvas, John Trumbull, 1822. Collection of the Office of the Architect of the Capitol. John Trumbull was a famous American painter of the late eighteenth and early nineteenth centuries. He was an officer in the Continental army and painted many scenes from the American Revolution. This image of General Burgoyne is a detail from a larger painting that shows General Burgoyne handing his sword to General Gates. This painting is one a series of four works by Trumbull that hang in the Rotunda of the Capitol in Washington, D.C. All show scenes from American history. **Page 12 (top).** *Screw-Barrel Pistol.* Brass, silver, and wood, c. 1770–1780. The George C. Neumann Collection at Valley Forge National Historic Park. This type of pistol would have been carried by an officer as his personal side arm. At this time, officers had to pay for their own uniforms and equipment. Screw-barrel pistols were so named because the barrel of the pistol was screwed off to load the bullet and the gunpowder. Rifles and muskets were loaded by pushing the bullet and the gunpowder down the barrel with a long rod. Screw-barrel pistols took longer to load than other types of guns. **Page 15 (left).** *Powder Horn.* Horn and brass, 1776. The George C. Neumann Collection at Valley Forge National Historic Park. Soldiers carried their personal supply of gunpowder in powder horns. The horns were often elaborately carved. A soldier who was a skilled carver might be paid by other soldiers to decorate their powder horns. Gunpowder was used to spark the explosion that pushed the bullet out of the gun. There were very few gunpowder factories in the colonies. Almost all of the gunpowder used by American soldiers during the Revolution came from France. **Page 16 (left).** *American Horseman's Saber.* Steel and ivory, c. 1770s. The George C. Neumann Collection at Valley Forge National Historic Park. A saber is a type of sword that has a slightly curved blade and was meant to be used on horseback. The steel blade was made in Germany, and the elephant ivory handle was made in the colonies. This sword could have belonged to either an officer or an ordinary soldier.

Web Sites

Due to the changing nature of Internet links, PowerKids Press has developed an online list of Web sites related to the subject of this book. This site is updated regularly. Please use this link to access the list:

www.powerkidslinks.com/afbar/saratoga/